I0815582

Theropods

Meat-Eating Dinosaurs

by Grace Hansen

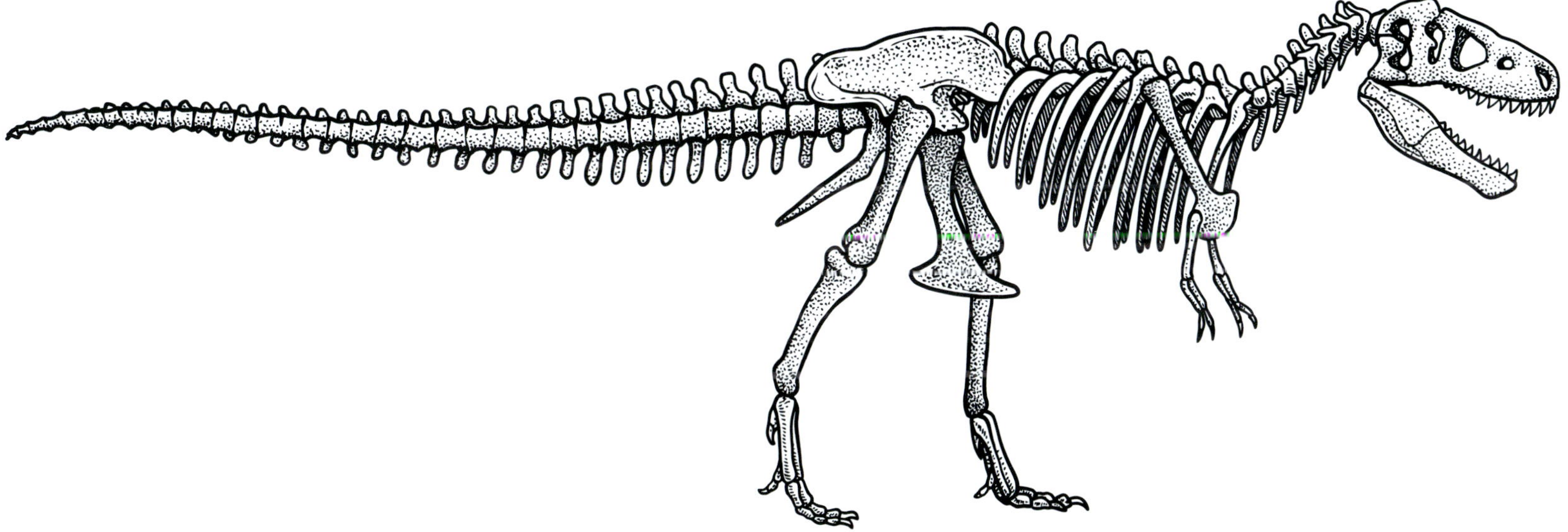

Abdo Kids Jumbo is an Imprint of Abdo Kids
abdobooks.com

abdobooks.com

Published by Abdo Kids, a division of ABDO, P.O. Box 398166, Minneapolis, Minnesota 55439.

Abdo Kids Jumbo™ is a trademark and logo of Abdo Kids.

Printed in the United States of America, North Mankato, Minnesota.

052025

092025

Photo Credits: Adobe Stock, Alamy, Getty Images, Science Source, Shutterstock

Production Contributors: Teddy Borth, Jennie Forsberg, Grace Hansen
Design Contributors: Victoria Bates, Candice Keimig

Library of Congress Control Number: 2024947602

Publisher's Cataloging-in-Publication Data

Names: Hansen, Grace, author.

Title: Theropods: meat-eating dinosaurs / by Grace Hansen

Other Title: meat-eating dinosaurs

Description: Minneapolis, Minnesota : Abdo Kids, 2026 | Series: Dinosaur groups | Includes online resources and index.

Identifiers: ISBN 9798384905196 (lib. bdg.) | ISBN 9798384905899 (ebook) | ISBN 9798384906247 (read-to-me ebook)

Subjects: LCSH: Dinosaurs--Juvenile literature. | Prehistoric animals--Juvenile literature. | Animals, Fossil--Juvenile literature. | Paleontology--Juvenile literature.

Classification: DDC 567.90--dc23

Table of Contents

The Meat-Eating Dinosaurs

Theropods were a group of dinosaurs. They lived from the Middle Triassic to the Late Cretaceous Period. They were found throughout the world.

Jurassic

201 million years ago

Cretaceous

145 million years ago

Theropods

Theropods were a **diverse** group of dinosaurs. They ranged greatly in size and what they looked like. However, all theropods moved on two feet.

The smallest theropods compared in size to a chicken or a crow. The largest could grow as long as a semitrailer!

Theropods lived in many different **habitats**. Smaller theropods may have lived in forests where they could find shelter and small **prey**. Larger theropods likely lived near rivers and in open areas with lots of room for hunting.

Theropods were **carnivores**. The smallest theropods ate insects and other small **invertebrates**. Some theropods ate fish. The largest theropods ate other dinosaurs.

Microraptor

Microraptor was one of the smallest known dinosaurs. It was feathered and had wings on its arms and legs. It ate small animals, such as fish, lizards, and insects.

Early Cretaceous
Fossils found in
Asia
As long as a
dalmatian
2.6 ft
(0.8 m) long
As heavy as a
bottle of water
2.2 lbs (1 kg)
Microraptor

Eodromaeus

Eodromaeus was one of the earliest living theropods. It would have lived about 230 million years ago!

Late Triassic
Fossils found in
South America
As long as a
hockey post is tall
4 ft (1.2 m) long
As heavy as a
tabby cat
10 lbs (4.5 kg)
Eodromaeus

Sinraptor

Sinraptor was likely the top **predator** in its community. It had a huge mouth with blade-like teeth. It had small but powerful arms. It was a great hunter.

Sinraptor
Late Jurassic
Fossils found in
Asia
As long as a
pontoon boat
25 ft (7.6 m) long
As heavy as a
bull
2,000 lbs
(907 kg)

Giganotosaurus

Giganotosaurus is known from only a few and small remains. It was one of the largest known land **carnivores**. It was taller and longer than *Tyrannosaurus rex*!

Early Cretaceous
Fossils found in
South America
As long as the width of
5 parking spaces
40 ft (12 m) long
As heavy as
2 hippos
17,600 lbs
(7,900 kg)
Giganotosaurus

Common Theropod Features

Early Theropods

- Moved on two feet
- Bird-like features
- Hollow bones
- Short arms
- Sharp teeth
- Three toes on each foot
- Some had feathers

Later Theropods

- Moved on two feet
- Long, powerful legs
- Short arms
- Large, curved teeth for biting flesh and bone
- Powerful jaws
- Larger skull and brain
- Most had skin covered in small, bumpy scales

Glossary

carnivore – an animal that eats the flesh of other animals.

diverse – of different kinds or sorts.

habitat – the natural home of an animal or a plant.

invertebrate – an animal that does not have a backbone or skeleton inside its body.

predator – an animal that hunts other animals for food.

prey – an animal that is hunted by other animals for food.

Index